To Sam

FRENCH ARROGANCE PROD
116, boulevard Saint-Germain | 75006 Paris

ISBN : 978-2-9566023-1-6

HOW TO BECOME A PARISIAN IN ONE HOUR?

Olivier GIRAUD

Illustrator : Solène DEBIÈS

FRENCH ARROGANCE PROD
PARIS

"I like the color as long as it's black"

Coco Chanel

CONTENTS

EDITORIAL

Welcome to Paris, the capital of France. 2.5 million inhabitants but... a single state of mind.
Since childhood, your parents raised you to be a "kind" human being, teaching you values such as simplicity, respect, punctuality, solidarity and politeness.
Close your eyes, take a deep breath and... forget all that!
Your new life in the Parisian jungle begins today!
For more than 10 years now, I have taught - and I am still teaching - almost a million people how to become a real Parisian through my show **"How to Become a Parisian in One Hour?"**

And today, you're my new student!

At the end of this training, you will become a true Parisian and at the same time, you will be hated throughout the world, and even more so in the Province (people living outside of Paris), because... yes... perfection is annoying! Also, it is likely that your parents will no longer recognise you.
Don't worry, it's completely normal: a visit (even a short one) to Paris will change you forever!

You can do it!

Your devoted teacher,

O. Giraud

1. THE CLICHÉS OF THE PARISIAN: MYTH OR REALITY?

MACARONS
Paris
Rue de
Rivoli

For decades, Parisians have had a very bad reputation. Far from displeasing us, this notoriety suits us perfectly and we are very proud of it!

If there was such a thing as a world championship of "the least welcoming inhabitants on the planet", we would take centre stage on the podium.

As a comedian, I've had the opportunity to visit many countries. Everywhere I've been, I've asked the natives of these places to describe Parisians.
From Thailand to Senegal, from the United States to India, from England to Ireland - the description of the Parisian doesn't change, their opinions are unanimous, and the adjectives they use to characterize Parisians are not always flattering!

So, is this negative image of the Parisian a myth or reality?

1. THE PARISIAN IS A FRENCH LOVER

FALSE!

Around the world, Parisians are stereotyped as romantic, French lovers.

A huge THANK YOU to Edith Piaf for contributing to the popularity of this image, but what is the reality today?

Nowadays, when you ask a Parisian about love, he will answer: ***"love, what you mean?"***

The Parisian has no time to fall in love.

That's why nearly half of all Parisians are single. However, single does not mean abstinent. Parisians are the champions of France when it comes to conquests, with 19 partners in their lifetime versus 11 in Province*. Romance is gradually disappearing to make way for recreational sex without a future (44% of male Parisians don't even know the name of their sexual partner, whilst women are more attentive at 17%*). So yes, Paris is the city of love...if you're looking for a one-night stand!

**Source: Ifop January 2017*

*** unknown*

2. THE PARISIAN IS ARROGANT

TRUE!

The Parisian is good-looking, elegant, slim, stylish, creative, cultured...and lives in the most beautiful city in the world. It would be such a pity to be modest!

3. THE PARISIAN IS SELFISH

TRUE!

How would you have time to think of others, when you don't have time to think of yourself?!

4. THE PARISIAN IS COLD AND ALOOF

TRUE!

Parisians don't have the time or the desire to be sociable. They don't have a second to lose: finding new friends is difficult when you don't have time for your current friends! If you really want to have a Parisian friend, you must be patient! The Parisian is not very trusting, and is on guard for a long time (about 5 years). Once trust is established, he or she becomes funny, endearing and above all; faithful. The Parisian is like a sea urchin: you work hard to remove the spines but the interior is often tasty!

5. THE PARISIAN ALWAYS POUTS

FALSE!

The Parisian is not pouting, his closed face is only the reflection of his life. You will quickly notice that he is strangely silent, despite his unhealthy stress levels.

It's quite rare to see him smile, except for his sadistic joy when a person gets stuck between the doors of the metro. The Parisian doesn't pretend to be happy, his depressive state is on full display:

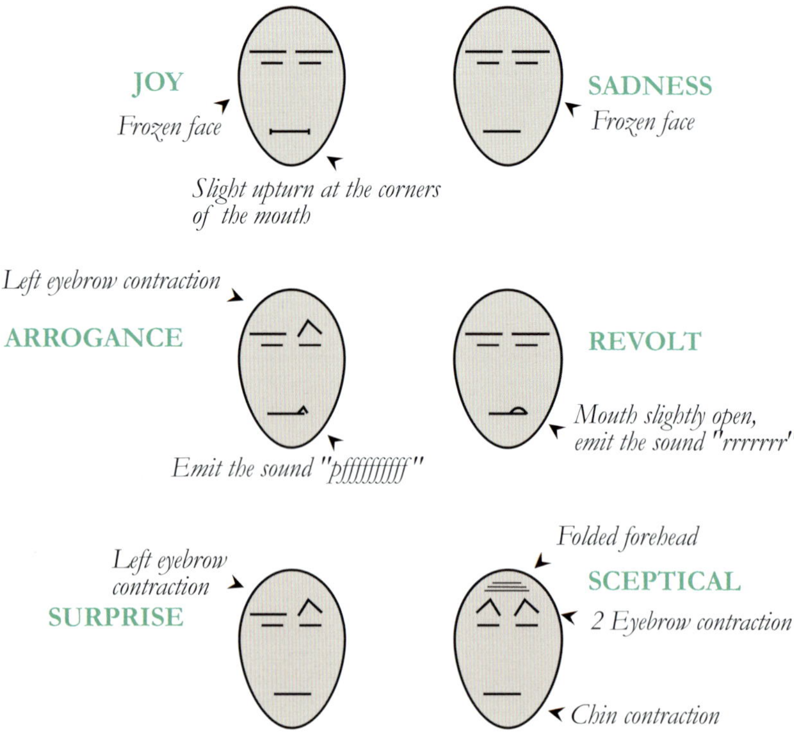

6. THE PARISIAN DOES NOT LIKE TOURISTS

TRUE!

The Parisian is not responsible for the beauty of his city, he has never asked the 30 million tourists a year to come and visit him! Why be warm with people who crowd the metro, walk at 2mph or ask for help without making the effort to speak French?
But tourists are tolerated... they remind Parisians of their superiority!

7. THE PARISIAN IS STRESSED

TRUE!

Obviously...
How can he not be? If he wasn't, he would be Icelandic!

8. THE PARISIAN HATES PROVINCE ACCENTS

TRUE!

The Parisian has no accent, but everyone else does! The more southern the accent is, the more murderous the Parisian feels.

cf Map next page →

WHAT PARISIANS THINK ABOUT "PROVINCE" ACCENTS ?

- THE REFERENCE
- Hilarious
- Your accent is so agressive, you're french, not german !
- You like drinking alcohol, but can you articulate ?
- Stop singing when you speak
- Farmers are working, they don't have time to speak !

9. THE PARISIAN IS BOBO

TRUE!

Not all Parisians are, but those who are, really are!
The term Bobo is a mixture of two terms, using the two first letters of each word: **BO**urgeois (rich and classy person) and **BO**hème (bohemian), two words that totally contradict each other!

Where do you find it?

In all districts, except the 6th, 7th, 8th and 16th arrondissement (bourgeois without la bohème).

How do you recognize the Bobo?

Easy: it looks neglected but damn stylish!

- He snacks on pumpkin seeds and gets drunk on organic Breton apple juice.
- He's revolted by junk food, but happy to eat a McChicken.
- He goes to work on a scooter or a bike to fight pollution, but will get on a plane 10 times a year - because Mauritius is great in January and the French Riviera is a must in June!
- He advocates a culture of sharing, although his best friend is a wealth manager who has taught him a great deal about tax exemption.
- He is against hyperconsumption despite buying the latest MacBook: it's much more convenient than sorting through photos on the latest iPhone.
- He is a fan of yoga and meditation but becomes hysterical when someone rides on the bicycle path!

10. THE PARISIAN IS A NICOTINE ADDICT

FALSE

One might think that stress causes people to smoke... well, no! Parisians are actually among those who smoke the least in France, with only 22% of smokers versus the French Riviera (32%), the east (30.1%), south east (30.3%), and the north (30.5%)*.

The Parisian lives life to the full, but does not want to see it go up in smoke...

** Source: Public Health Survey France, May 2018.*

11. THE PARISIAN IS SLIM

TRUE!

It's a certainty, even! If you dare to visit the Province, you realize that the sedentary lifestyle of the Provincials fill every fold of their jeans.

The bustling Parisian life eliminates each calorie consumed.

To draw a real conclusion, let's compare energy expenditure between Parisians and Provincials:

PROVINCE	
Walking 80 metres a day	**2 calories**
Preparing a cocktail	**4 calories**
Refilling a cocktail glass	**1 calorie**
Picking cherry tomatoes in a vegetable garden	**1 calorie**
Looking for a job	**18 calories**
Network searching (3G or 4G)	**8 calories**
Smoking	**21 calories**
Waiting for the TV news	**7 calories**
Watching TV	**49 calories**

PARIS	
6 km walk a day*	**400 calories**
Running after the metro	**46 calories**
Avoiding dog excrement	**22 calories**
Climbing 120 steps	**89 calories**
Going down 120 steps	**68 calories**
Climbing 22 steps of the broken down escalator	**12 calories**
Raising your hand 20 times to get a coffee	**8 calories**
Raising your hand 20 times to pay for your coffee	**8 calories**
Waiting for change	**8 calories**
Criticizing passers-by	**199 calories**
Looking for a terrace seat in the sun	**22 calories**
Avoiding Amnesty International volunteers	**78 calories**

Do not waste your time counting calories, the verdict is final! This is how the Parisian is able to eat at a restaurant and drink until he blacks out, without gaining a single ounce of fat.

**RATP statistics January 2016*

12. *LA PARISIENNE* IS SENSUAL AND GLAMOROUS

FALSE!

You think that the Parisienne bites into a rose flavoured macaron as soon as she wakes up, then puts on a little black dress, slips her freshly pedicured feet into beautiful high heels, then runs along the cobblestoned streets of Saint-Germain-des-Prés with incredible class. You're wrong!

Thanks anyway to the perfume advertisers who have maintained this myth for generations, but the Parisian woman is not Coco Chanel!

The Parisienne is a woman like all others. She wakes up with puffy eyes and a pillow mark on her cheek - courtesy of the bad quality champagne she drank the night before. She takes the metro at rush hour, gets angry, moans, insults, gets insulted and eats a ham sandwich at noon (or 80g of edamame bean salad with smoked tofu for vegans). She dresses in clothes from the big chains (often at final reduction) or in second-hand stores.

The lucky ones are out of cash on the 10th of each month, the others on the 5th. However, they all have the "Parisian attitude": a mixed cocktail of arrogance, coldness, disdain, sufficiency and elegance.

THE EXCEPTION

Her name is
Laura or Céline,
in her forties,
product manager
for a major luxury brand
or influencer.
You can see her on
the terrace, on a chic avenue
in the 8th arrondissement.
Any other evidence?
Look at her plate,
she orders a salad with
the sauce on the side
over and over again.

Now that you have a clearer vision of the Parisian, you are finally ready to begin your training on how to become the "perfect Parisian".

Having just arrived in Paris, you face your biggest challenge yet: to find an apartment!

2. ACCOMMODATION IN PARIS

- *Wait two minutes, I'm just finishing the meal.*

THIS PART IS INTENDED
FOR MIDDLE-CLASS READERS.
THE RICH CAN GO DIRECTLY
TO THE THIRD PART!

Ah...Paris, the most beautiful city in the world... Its beautiful buildings, its magnificent zinc rooftops...

Every morning, you wake up in a 200m2 apartment, enjoy your coffee on the terrace… STOP dreaming!
Unless you earn at least 40k euros a year, your search for an apartment will be a real nightmare!

I wish you the very best of luck!

FINANCIAL CONDITIONS

If you make a good living and your parents are cardiologists, choose a real estate agency; they will be waiting for you with open arms!
But if your salary is not stupendous and your parents are ruined by private consultations at the cardiologist, you should try websites that connect you to landlords directly (leboncoin.com, pap.com etc...).
If you're not able to afford living in central Paris, another option is the suburbs... although a "real" Parisian would rather die than live in the suburbs. The choice is yours!

Important tip: if your salary is not great, put yourself in a relationship. Love will come afterwards (or not)!

Before you do endless research, don't forget that you have to:

- Earn at least 3 times the rent per month
- Be on a permanent contract
- Have 1 or 2 guarantors

If you fail to satisfy one or more of these criteria, you will have to resort to apartment sharing or living in Province.

LOOKING FOR A PIECE OF ROOF

As early as 6am, check your inbox for the property alerts you have previously activated.
To interpret the ads correctly, you must understand all the terms used in French:

- ***Location*** **(Rent)**: Crazy amount of money paid to a landlord in exchange for housing. When someone says to you: "Renting an apartment is like throwing money out the window!" Slap him, and ask him to give you 200,000 euros for the purchase of an $18m^2$ studio apartment.

- ***Studio***: Minimalist surface space that includes kitchen, bathroom, bedroom and toilet. All in one room.
If you enjoy making love with your head banging against the

fridge, you will be satisfied.
Price: between 700 and 1400 euros per month.

• ***Studette:*** Even smaller than a studio. Does Tetris give you nostalgia? Go for it! The only difference between a *studette* and a prison cell is 500 euros per month.

• ***Kitchenette:*** Mini kitchen, mini oven, mini fridge, big frustration.

• ***Mezzanine*** **(mezzanine floor):** Wooden surface, accessible by stairs or a ladder, added between the ceiling and the floor. Not recommended if you're tall, unless your partner is an osteopath.

• ***Toilettes sur le palier*** **(Toilets on the landing):** Old-fashioned Parisian charm that forces you to leave your home to go to the toilets. A way to know your neighbours well. A great moment of sharing and intimacy. If you're suffering from cystitis, the sink will be your best friend!

• ***Caution solidaire*** **(Guarantor):** Mandatory document when the owner thinks that you are less than nothing. It can be parents or family. The guarantor agrees to pay your rent if you can no longer afford it.

• ***Caution*** **(Deposit):** Amount of money (equal to the rent) to be paid to the landlady. It allows her to heck that you have immediate cash but especially to guard against damage to housing or make up for unpaid rent (1 month deposit for an unfurnished home and 2 months for a furnished apartment). The money is returned at the end of your lease (theoretically!).

• ***Colocation* (apartment-sharing):** A lifestyle imposed by lack of money; you share a flat with one or several roommates to reduce the cost of rent.

• ***Colocation avec personne âgée* (Flat sharing with a senior):** You live with a senior in a house or an apartment and you listen to his pain. Good (but annoying) way to save money!

• ***Dossier* (file):** Administrative and financial autobiography to prove that you are a person of trust. Preparation time: 2 weeks (2 years if you are messy).

• ***Ascenseur* (elevator):** Vertical lifting device which is very important, because the majority of Parisian buildings have 6 or 7 floors. If (unfortunately) you live on the top floor without an elevator, your daily life will be (very) sporty! User of the Tinder app? Warn your future conquests that you'll need a shower before making love.

Now that you are familiar with the French real estate vocabulary, it is time to pre-select the apartments that interest you.
If you're looking for an apartment, you have to be very expressive! After reading each ad, exclaim:

"Oh, putain, c'est cher !" ("Oh, damn it's expensive!")

As soon as an apartment includes at least one of your criteria, call the landlord or the agency and arrange a viewing appointment.

THE VISIT

On D-day, try to be classy; you must reassure the owner. How will you take care of the apartment if you do not take care of yourself?

(If you're a punk, at least come without your dog).
When you arrive at the address of the appointment, do not be surprised that there are already 40 people lined up at the door (yes, you're not the only one!), but don't hesitate to overtake them! First come, first served! Politeness has never offered a roof over your head!
During the visit, keep smiling even if you want to hang yourself. Your salary does not allow you to be demanding.

At the end of the visit, give them your documents and compliment the landlord by telling him that his apartment is beautiful.
A few days later, your phone rings, and the landlord tells you that you're the lucky winner... You have just overcome the biggest challenge in your life - be proud of yourself! You finally live in PARIS, you have become a "real" Parisian...

LAST CHANCE...

If you think that your precarious situation prevents you from finding accommodation, do not hesitate to falsify some information or documents, such as an employment contract or letter of recommendation; and give them your mother's phone number, who will act as your employer or banker at the time of the call! Better to be dishonest than to be homeless.
After all, what's the risk? 3 years in prison is much cheaper than rent!

You finally have a (bad) place to live! Now it's time to enjoy the city. Let's start by teaching you how to adopt the Parisian look!

3. THE PARISIAN LOOK

- Are you looking for a size ?
- No, I'm just looking.

Oh, Paris… the capital of fashion and elegance… Chanel, Dior, Louis Vuitton, Louboutin, Jean-Paul Gaultier... Calm down!

Paris is the capital of fashion... 2 weeks a year! The rest of the year, the majority of Parisians are more like your cousin from Manchester than our first lady Brigitte Macron.
Only a fraction of the population makes an effort to dress well. Still, with no less than 8000 clothes shops, you will find a way to make your dressing room overflow!

Let's go!

DRESS CODE

If your wardrobe is full of brightly coloured clothes, put them in a plastic bag and give them to charity! Parisians wear black because black is classy! If you're a little eccentric, opt for grey or dark blue.

Men
Jeans, t-shirt, fitted shirt, polo, white trainers, slightly worn.

Women
Just arrived in Paris, you will have to choose a side:

- **The "classic" Parisian**

Black jeans or black trousers, skirts or dresses only during a heat wave. ALERT! Fashion faux pas: never wear a mini skirt! Parisian girls are French, not English! Classic blouse or black top.
Very important detail: if it's cold, wear a scarf and if it's hot... wear a scarf!

- **The "trendy" Parisian**

As a fan of fashion magazines, the trendy Parisienne is on the lookout for all the novelties and new trends. In her wardrobe, the self-respecting Parisienne has the following essentials: trench coat, leather jacket, loose-fit blouse, la petite robe noire "little black dress", cashmere jumper, Jeans, *marinière* (striped shirt, white and dark blue), men's shirt, *escarpins* (black leather shoes, with high (but not too high) heels! only one accessory (earrings, hat, designer bag) Simply chic!

If your income doesn't allow you to buy designer gear, then be creative!
Go to the ***"vide dressing"*** (where you can buy relatively affordable second-hand designer clothes).
Fashion either reinvents itself, or goes full circle. The shops in the Marais district offer clothes at unbeatable prices! Buy by the kilo and wait for the dresses that looks like curtains to be back fashion!

WHERE TO GO SHOPPING ?

You like:

• Designer clothes and socks that cost 300 euros/pair: The triangle d'or (golden triangle) or the 8th arrondissement (Avenue Montaigne, Avenue Georges V and Champs-Elysees), rue du Faubourg Saint-Honoré.

• Chain stores: rue de Rivoli, the market halls, rue de Rennes.

• Small designers and second-hand clothes shops: Le Marais.

• Old designers: 16th arrondissement.

• If you're "Made in CHINA": Haussmann and Opera.

WHEN TO GO SHOPPING ?

Before you walk through the doors of a store, you should know that the Parisian and especially the Parisian woman loves a bargain! She refuses to pay full price for an item that will be on sale in a few weeks anyway.

Two options are available to you:

- **Sales:**

For several months each year, the sales in Paris cause an urban battlefield. The civil war lasts 4 weeks, twice a year (winter and summer).
To find your happiness, the technique is simple. Take a day off for the opening day of the sales. On D-day, try to arrive well before your favourite store opens. Barely open, rush towards the shelves and let your lowest instincts run free; it's now or never!
If two of you get your hands on the same item, make sure to forcefully pull it out of her hands! Is she still not giving up? Tear off a lock of her hair; fair play can wait....
Congratulations, you leave with this yellow t-shirt sold at 70% discount. It's much too big, but the saleswoman has assured you that it will shrink in the first wash...

If you are agoraphobic or if you don't have the courage to fight for a t-shirt, here's another option:

• **Private Sales:**

This makes you feel ultra privileged! Your favourite store gives you an exclusive invitation to enjoy great discounts a few days before the sale starts. WOW, isn't that great?
To be part of it, no stress! Nothing is easier: select your favourite stores, then give your email address to the cashier. Don't worry, you will always be invited, and in return, she will be happy to sell your personal information to insurance and telephone companies.

HOW TO BEHAVE LIKE A REAL PARISIAN IN A SHOP?

As soon as you enter the shop, avoid saying hello to the salesperson, because she'll think you're weird or a tourist.
Rummage quickly through the shelves; you're not here to hang out!

If the salesperson offers to help, direct the palm of your hand towards her and say: ***"Non, je regarde !"*** ("No, I'm looking!").

If you have a question, don't ask anyone - you can read the labels! Don't hesitate to unfold the stack of clothes to find your size. If your research is futile, go looking for the salesperson, and don't forget to complain out loud:
"Putain, elles sont jamais là quand on en a besoin"
("Fuck, they are never there when we need them").

95% of the time, she will say: ***"tout est en rayon"*** ("everything is on the shelf"). Raise your eyes and sigh.
Don't thank her because she did nothing for you!

If you find what you are looking for, go to the fitting rooms. The salesperson will point you in the right direction with a chin movement.
After a few endless minutes of waiting, a fitting room finally becomes available....
Never ask the salesperson for advice: without even looking at you, despite the fact that you look like a chicken in a condom, she will say: ***"Ça vous va bien !"*** ("It looks good on you!").
Don't forget that a salesperson is not your private stylist! She's not here to show you off, she's just hoping you get out of her store as soon as possible!

If you like the clothes, head to the cash register and its long queue. Take the opportunity to complain aloud:
"Putain, c'est pas possible d'avoir qu'une caisse ouverte !"
("Damn, can you believe there's only one till open!").
Pay and leave the store without saying goodbye!

Congratulations!
You can now leave the house and not be laughed at!

Why don't we go and celebrate
your new look at the restaurant?

4. THE RESTAURANT

- We have 20 minutes to eat because we have a real job !

Ah, Paris... the city of simple (and expensive) pleasures: a café allongé (espresso diluted with hot water) lying on the terrace, a passion fruit mojito on a roof-top, a salmon tartar with yuzu in an ephemeral restaurant, a charcuterie board and a glass of red wine in a local bistro....

Ah, Paris... the city of simple (and expensive) pleasures: a café allongé (espresso diluted with hot water) lying on the terrace, a passion fruit mojito on a roof-top, a salmon tartar with yuzu in an ephemeral restaurant, a charcuterie board and a glass of red wine in a local bistro....
With no less than 5000 bars and more than 20,000 restaurants, the City of Light is a paradise for gourmets and bourgeois alcoholics*alike.
Parisians are testers of new concepts, always making new discoveries they can't wait to share with their entourage:
"You must check out that amazing new Bò bún place in the 10th! "

Self-respecting Parisians (who have the means to do so) go to the restaurant at least once a week. However, the Parisian watches his waistline. He doesn't eat much but he eats well!
Important information: Parisians are volunteer food critics. They are highly demanding on the quality of the cuisine and uncompromising on the speed of service.
Parisian servers and customers have the reputation of being the most unpleasant on the planet!

*Parisian who goes out at least 5 nights a week. A fan of the expression: ***"It's okay, you only have one life"***, he never refuses a glass of alcohol.

Don't hesitate to make life difficult for the waiter; he's already ready to do the same for you.
Enjoy your meal!

APERITIF ON THE TERRACE

To start your evening off right, go have a drink in a bar. Most offer a happy hour (buy one, get one free, or discounts on drinks). Whether it's 2 or 30 degrees, sit on the terrace. If you're a smoker, your neighbours will undoubtedly be disturbed by your smoke. Ignore them if they're not happy, all they have to do is take refuge inside.

Before ordering your drink, check the time on your phone to make sure that happy hour is not over - the waiter will not be generous for one more second!

Enjoy your drink! If you're hungry, order a plate of cold cuts. If you're vegan, olives marinated in thyme will do the trick!
Barely finished, head for the restaurant!

What do Parisians drink?

- **WOMEN**

Strawberry mojito, Aperol spritz, white wine or rosé

- **MEN**

Red wine, beer and whisky

RESTAURANT

Which neighbourhood to choose?

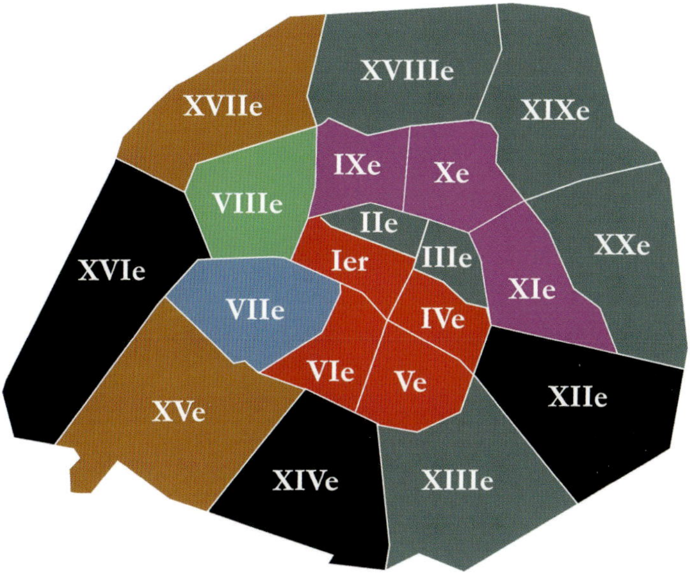

- You like chic and expensive atmospheres
- You're familiar with wealth tax and you drink more champagne than water
- You like money and rich people
- You eat organic, gluten-free, you like manuka honey and you like being surrounded by parisian Bobo
- You have 3 or 4 children and you don't want to be far from home, stay in your neighbourhood
- You like sad and quiet neighborhoods
- You like cool and popular neighborhoods

PRATICAL INFORMATIONS

When to go there?

• **Lunch**

From Monday to Friday, the businesspeople and their impatience arrive at 1pm.

Saturday and especially Sunday is BRUNCH! The Parisian considers this meal a true religion!

The ceremony is celebrated at:

 Model parents with children

 Selfish parents with children

 Couples without children or with children but who regret having them

 Freshly sobered singles

Which dish to eat:

Eggs Benedict with smoked salmon or maple syrup pancakes and mimosa (champagne + orange juice) - this is the only meal of the week where alcoholism is trendy!

• **Dinner**

From Thursday evening to Saturday, from 9pm.

THE ARRIVAL

If you have booked a table, be no more than 10 minutes late.
As soon as you arrive, go to a table that has not yet been cleared... it annoys the waiter, but if the table has already been occupied, it must be fine!
As soon as you sit down, spot the waiter and mime with your hands: ***"LE MENU!"*** ("the menu")

ORDERING

After ignoring you for ages, the waiter finally gets to your table.
If he offers you an aperitif, answer him: ***"On prendra du vin !"*** ("We'll have wine!").
You're not a tourist, you know very well that 2 cocktails cost the same as a bottle of wine.
Be careful, as soon as the waiter asks you the closed question: ***"Eau plate ou gazeuse ?"*** ("Still or sparkling water?"), answer openly: ***"Non, une carafe d'eau"*** ("No, tap water"). You look like a poor customer but you just saved 7 euros.

When you're ready to order, stare at the waiter and raise your hand! If he is late in taking the order, call the reception of the restaurant:
"Bonsoir, je suis le client installé depuis plus de 20 minutes à la table 18, pourriez-vous dire à notre serveur que l'on se sent vieillir ?"*
("Good evening, I'm the client who's been sitting at table 18 for more than 20 minutes, could you tell our server that we're sitting here getting old?"). It's rude, but it works!

**true story, and I was the waiter*

As he approaches the table, take the menu back in hand - you're ready but you still need some time to think! The waiter will tell you: ***"Je reviens dans quelques minutes"*** ("I'll be back in a few minutes"). Don't let him go, he'll never come back.

If you are not sure of your choice, avoid asking him: ***"Qu'est ce que vous me recommandez ?"*** ("What do you recommend?"), because he will tell you about the dishes he has to sell quickly or those that bring the boss a nice profit margin.

When your choice is made, complicate the task; Parisians don't have a reputation for being easy.
Don't be surprised if the waiter raises his left eyebrow and emits a pfff, if you ask him:
"Je suis allergique au gluten, mais j'adore les pâtes! Qu'est ce que vous me recommandez ?" ("I'm allergic to gluten, but I love pasta! What do you recommend?")

"Est ce que je pourrais avoir mon faux-filet bien cuit mais pas trop, avec du rouge au milieu, mais pas de sang ?" ("Could I have my New York strip well done but not too much, red in the middle, but no blood?")

"Je vais prendre le saumon à l'unilatéral, mais j'aime pas la fondue de poireau. C'est possible d'avoir la garniture du cabillaud à la place ?" ("I'm going to have the salmon, but I don't like leek fondue. Is it possible to have the cod garnish instead?")
"Vous avez des plats vegan ?" ("Do you have any vegan dishes?")

THE WAIT

Once the order is placed, raise your hand and ask for a basket of bread. As soon as he brings it to you, ask for a *carafe d'eau* (tap water), then ask for bread again. It's free and it's filling!

Chances are the wait will be endless. In that case, stare at the waiter and as soon as he looks at you, open your eyes wide, wrinkle your forehead, and mime the Y from YMCA's choreography. He will quickly understand that you are on the verge of implosion.

If you eat on the terrace, you will see a rose seller more often than the waiter. If you want to impress a Parisian woman, NEVER buy her these roses. In Paris, they are referred to as "gutter roses", as the seller refreshes them in the gutter before selling them. So trust me, she will much rather prefer it if you jokingly told the seller "No thanks, she's just my wife!"

THE TASTING

Your dish finally arrives... check that it's hot. If it's just warm, don't hesitate to tell the waiter! Once your dish is heated up, wait a few minutes because it's now too hot (the cook is vengeful)...
Take a picture of it and share it on social media. Enrage your friends with these 4 hashtags:
#hardlife #bonappetit #instagood #instafood.

Enjoy your meal without forgetting to criticize the portion size, seasoning and presentation. A few strokes of the fork later, ask for the dessert menu, even if you're already planning to get the tiramisu with several spoons.

The other option is "le café gourmand" (gourmet coffee): coffee, preferably long, served with 3 or 4 mini portions of desserts for the modest sum of 10 euros. The restaurant owner empties his fridge and you… you're so happy...

A COFFEE AND L'ADDITION (THE BILL)

You don't have a sweet tooth? Order only *un café allongé* (American coffee) and the bill!
If your coffee doesn't arrive, ask the waiter: ***"Vous êtes partis le chercher en Colombie ?"*** ("Did you go to Colombia to get it?"). Don't expect to make him laugh because he's already heard it a thousand times, though his exasperation will give you one last little pleasure.

Once you've necked your coffee, ask for the bill a second time. After the third time, you get up and pay at the bar instead. Tips are at the discretion of the customer, so be discreet and don't give him anything!

Congratulations, you have successfully passed the restaurant stage! Ready for the next one?

You must now go home!
Choose the most economical way,
the metro.

5 . THE METRO

PSY
S'ouvrir aux autres
PHILOSOPHIE
La notion de partage
Solène Debiès

The metro is the most popular means of transport used by Parisians. Every day, more than 5 million passengers use its underground network.

The metro and its 16 lines (20 in 2030) remain the fastest and most efficient way to travel around Paris.

During the week, opening hours pretty much follow the daily rhythm of the population. Parisians start work around 9:30 am, so it's logical for the first metro to start at 5:30 am. In the evening, the last metro leaves at 00:30 while the bars close at 2am...

On weekends and bank holidays, RATP (**R**egie **A**utonome des **T**ransports **P**arisiens) offers you an extra hour in the evening, which is very useful when you want to forget your week and enjoy a few vodka shots.

Be ready for a unique experience...

Are you ready?

Let's do it!

WHAT PARISIANS THINK OF PARISIAN METRO LINES

- 1 Rich people, businesspeople, tourists and pickpockets
- 2 Sexe, drugs and Montmartre
- 3 It's long, it's so long!
- 3bis Useless
- 4 Only appreciated by sardines!
- 5 If you like traffic regulations
- 6 Magic when passing in front of the Eiffel Tower
- 7 Opera, Louvre and Galeries Lafayette
- 7bis Useless bis
- 8 Endless
- 9 No one has ever understood the difference between this one and line 8
- 10 If you are rich and not in a hurry
- 11 It's dirty, so dirty!
- 12 Sad people who go to sad places...
- 13 Hell, purgatory, disgrace
- 14 Absolute perfection

METRO PARIS
13
7
5
4
12
7bis
11
3bis
14
6
3
9
2
1
10
8

WELCOME TO THE JUNGLE "100 FEET UNDER"

Before you run down the few steps that separate you from the security gate, you need to think like a Parisian: you are entering an area of lawlessness and you will therefore act accordingly.
If, unfortunately, you have to recharge your monthly pass or buy a single ticket, leave your home 10 minutes earlier, because the automatic machines are always crowded with people trying to understand how they work.

A ticket will cost you 1.90 euros, but the real Parisian opts for a monthly pass (pass Navigo), with half the cost covered by her employer.
In order to optimize your time, slap the bag or wallet against the magnetic terminal.

If a fraudster tailgates you through the security gate, let him do it - and hope that the controllers are waiting for him around the corner. That is always entertaining!

Once you get to the metro corridors, walk really fast. With a little practice, you will adopt the slalom technique that will save you some time by overtaking lost tourists. If an old lady slows you down, don't hesitate to shout at her : ***"Degage la vieille !"***
("Out of the way, old lady!"). Use her state of shock as an opportunity to overtake her!

During your journey, you must pay attention to the various noises. If you hear a braking noise, prepare for a deep exhale as this means a 50/50 chance of the metro arriving at the platform, imminently! This is an orgasmic moment for a Parisian!

If you missed your chance and just watched the metro go by under your nose (French expression), consider it a real failure. It will help you refine your slalom technique for next time.

Then take a look at the sign that tells you how long you have to wait for the next train. As a real Parisian, this is how you'll feel when you see the waiting times:

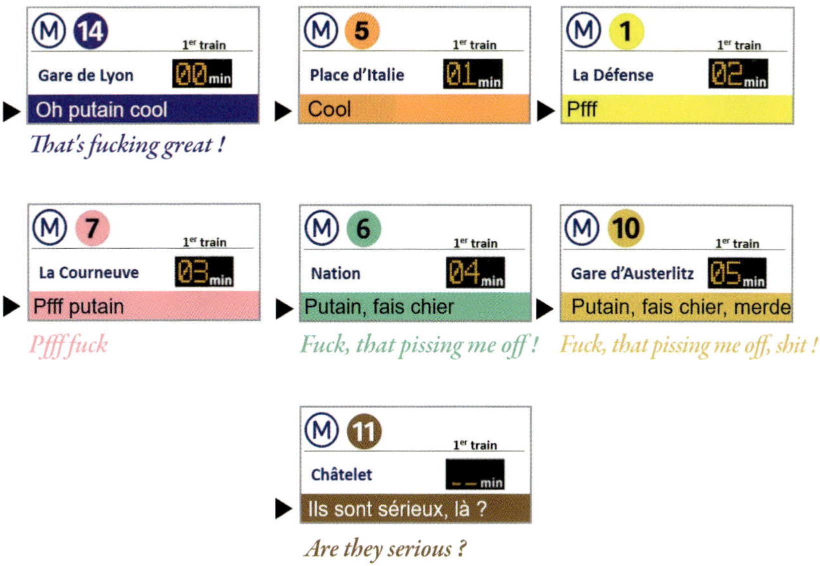

Whatever your waiting time; Paris, the world capital of perfume, will surprise you. It is quite possible that the smell of urine, macerated sweat and poo may come up your nose. Don't gag, this is the underbelly of Paris.

LOOKING FOR AN AVAILABLE SEAT....

If you think you've completed the hardest part so far, think again! The metro just arrived, the doors are ready to open. From this moment on you have to be a good strategist.
The first objective is very clear: sitting down.

The strategy is simple: stay on the side of the door. As soon as it opens, don't wait for people to come out, just push everyone and rush to a free seat. You will probably be insulted, but it is better to be hated and seated than polite and standing.

If the carriage is already full when the doors open, don't hesitate for a second: YOU GET IN. Better to die than to wait for the next one!
Once inside, be careful, a pickpocket can strike at any time. He is very easy to recognize: his hands are always in his pockets, except that they are never his.

The biggest mistake is to rush to the *strapontin* (folding seat). If you get a high volume of traffic, you'll be the first to get up and comfort will be short-lived.

If a rude person decides to remain seated on it, you have to make sure everyone notices:
"Il voit pas qu'il y a du monde celui-là, Il ne peut pas se lever ?"
("Can't he see that it's crowded? Can't he get up?").

If you have found a seat, CONGRATULATIONS! If you're wondering if there is a perfect seat, the answer is yes! As soon as you enter the train, you will see (on your left or right), 2 times 4 seats. Choose the one on the window side, in the direction of travel! It is a real pleasure to see other passengers living a nightmare whilst you're comfortably seated in your **V**ery **I**ntelligent **P**arisian seat!
If you're dreaming of a week of rest at home with a solid viral infection, stand at the vertical metal bar, and your dream will quickly come true!

Once seated, here's a table of classic mistakes to avoid:

Mistakes	**Why**
Looking at yourself in the window of the carriage	The reflection of your face under the white neon light will remind you of your aunt Martine in palliative care.
Talking to your neighbour	You have no desire to meet him... the metro is not a meeting place!
Looking at the old lady smiling at you	She only wants your seat!
Paying attention to a pregnant woman	You're not responsible for her pregnancy; she played and now she's paying for it!
Being delighted by the presence of musicians in the train	There are a lot of singers on the metro. If you give them attention, they think you'll give them money. Ignore them! A Parisian doesn't like poor quality music! Only tourists and provincials will have a good time!

A few seconds before you reach your destination, get ready to exit the train. It is very likely that someone behind you will tell you, before your stop:
"PARDON, je dois descendre" ("Excuse me, I have to get off"). Turn around, and answer him: ***"Beh moi aussi!"*** ("Well, so do I!"). The same if someone asks you this whilst you're in the tunnel: ***"Vous descendez ?"*** ("Are you getting off?"),
reply: ***"Jamais entre 2 stations !"*** ("Never between two stations!").

The metro stops and it's time to get off. Shout ***"PARDON"*** ("excuse-me"), three times, louder and louder. If that's not enough, push everyone and don't forget to exclaim:
"Qu'est ce qu'ils sont cons ces gens !" ("These people are so stupid!").

SO CLOSE TO THE EXIT

On the platform, you'll likely see a woman with a stroller at the bottom of the stairs. Be careful, it's a trap... she is waiting for you! Look at your watch, hurry up and climb the stairs 2 by 2, don't even look at her!
If you're lucky and there's a working escalator; take it!
Don't stand still on the right and walk on the left. The escalator is not a means of transport, but a means of acceleration.
If a tourist or a provincial stands to the left, a simple ***"Rrrrrrrrr"*** (throat clearance) will be enough for him to move. As soon as you overtake him, look at him from the corner of your eye, and let out a ***"pffff"***.

With the exit approaching comes the last physical test: pushing the metal doors. Be careful: the RATP is very playful, only 1 door out of 3 works, it's up to you to find the right one! If you're in a teasing mood and have a few seconds, try this evil little game: When you push the metal doors, turn around, if you see a person 20 meters behind you, hold the door with a slight smile, he will start running so as not to waste your time! So enjoyable!

THE PARISIAN METRO, SO ROMANTIC...

If you're a woman, you will unfortunately be confronted with men in need of love:

1/ Rubber: a completely crazy man who mostly operates on the metro. He takes a strange pleasure in sticking his private parts against your buttocks, hoping with all his heart that the train will suddenly brake. If you're in this situation, move your rear end against a window and insult him! Don't yell: ***"A l'aide !"*** ("Help!"), because nobody cares...

2/ Perverse poet: someone closer to an animal than a human being, who considers you a piece of meat. First, he will approach you with poetic words in order to flatter you: ***"Oh, t'es bonne !"*** ("Oh, you're fucking hot"). Ignore him. You will then be entitled to a repartee such as: ***"De toute manière, t'es pas belle, s***** !"*** ("Well, you're an ugly b*****! anyway").

What irritates the Parisian in the metro:

- A signal failure.
- A tourist who sticks his big backpack in your face.
- A travel incident (RATP side)=someone threw themselves under the train.
- A young woman screaming on the phone: Hello, hello, hello, can you hear me? (No, he can't hear you but... we do!)
- A child who, at each stop, asks her parents for the number of remaining stations. Even more unbearable when parents count them!
- A bunch of Provincials who keep saying, ***"I could never live here!"*** (Good, it's already sold out!).
- The deafening sound of the doors closing.
- A couple of bobo vegans who enter the train with their 3 Yucca palms and 20 kilos of fertilized organic soil.
- A station closed because of a forgotten suitcase.
- Traffic interrupted due to passengers on the tracks! (Wow, what a great idea)
- A person who jumps on the train as the doors close. Even more annoying when he's proud of it!

The metro test is over. Well done, you survived!
If you don't have the courage to go through this painful experience again, choose another option: a taxi!

6 . THE TAXI

- 24, boulevard Poissonnière

- Sorry, it doesn't suit me, I'm not going that way !

In some cities around the world, taking a taxi is a real pleasure.
In New York, for example, they use the expression "jump in a taxi"!

In Paris, despite the 20,000 taxis, you don't jump in a taxi... You are desperately looking for one...
It will take a lot of patience and self-control to survive this experience.
Courage !

HOW TO DESCRIBE A TAXI DRIVER?

The Parisian taxi driver, commonly known as a "taxi", is often a man (93%) of a certain age, closer to being buried than to obtaining his driving licence.
After hundreds of thousands of miles on his meter, the taxi becomes antisocial, aggressive, grumpy and no longer speaks French, he simply grumbles!
In debt for decades to pay his license at 200,000 euros, he is unfortunately forced to work!

HOW TO FIND A TAXI DRIVER

- **Option 1 (not recommended):**

If you want to wait a few hours at the taxi stand surrounded by drunk Parisians screaming: ***"Putain, j'en peux plus d'attendre !"*** ("Fuck, I can't wait any longer!"), choose this option.

- **Option 2 (not recommended):**

Do you have too much money and you don't know what to do with it anymore? Order a taxi from the Parisian taxi booking office, it will arrive with 30 euros already on the meter... Don't try to guess where it came from..... You already have the answer; they are screwing you!

- **Option 3 (not recommended):**

A taxi is not allowed to stop outside the taxi stands... But don't worry, they all do!
If you see people on the pavement getting impatient, they are most likely waiting for a taxi! And yes, you weren't the only one with that idea!

Use a dishonest but great technique: as soon as you see a free taxi (green light), run as fast as you can to overtake all the poor honest people who are waiting patiently. Respectful human beings have never brought anyone home!

When a taxi finally stops, get directly into the back seat, covered with old, crusty leather. If the door is locked, it's probably because he doesn't like your destination! Don't be surprised if he says to you: ***"C'est pas ma route !"*** ("it's not on my route!")

On the other hand, if you wear a miniskirt and display a generous cleavage, he will be happy to drive you, as his testosterone level will take control of his revenues.

After a few minutes of negotiation, you are finally in the taxi:

Don't be surprised that the driver is as friendly as a Saudi prison door (French expression)... he is paid to drive you, not to entertain you.
Taxi drivers love music, so if you like jazz, you'll have an amazing time... If not, never ask him to change it, because it's his car!

Some taxis are adept at the "Shanghai Road". This is an unjustified detour inflicted on the customer by an indelicate driver, in order to make him pay the high price.
Check the counter every 10 seconds and get nervous when you are stuck in a traffic jam.

When you get to your destination, it's time to pay! The driver will tell you that:

- the card machine is down.
- cheques are not accepted.
- payments are cash only.

He will add that he doesn't have change, so that you can answer him: ***"c'est bon, gardez-la"*** ("It's okay, keep it!").
Don't fall into his trap, wait a few seconds, he'll find it. The taxi has more than one trick in his trunk.

When you get out of the car, slam the door and say,
"Qu'est ce qu'ils sont cons ces taxis !"
("What the hell are with these taxis?!"),
hoping you will never need one again...until next time.

ALTERNATIVE TO TAXIS

A few years ago, VTC (Véhicule de Tourisme avec Chauffeur) (Uber and few others) offered an impeccable service compared to taxis.
They welcomed you in 3-piece suits, greeted you by opening the door, offered you a bottle of water, candy, a phone charger… and you could even choose your music...
What a luxury!
Today, things have changed. The service remains cordial but the welcome gifts are long gone.

The prices of VTCs are essentially the same as the taxis, but beware of increases in the evening and on weekends. 50 euros from Champs Elysees to Concorde?! No thanks!

7. CLUBBING IN PARIS

- Do you really think you're gonna get me with a drink?

Ah... the magic of Paris... At night, the city of light turns into a temple of celebration, combining excess, transgression and madness. We sing, we dance, we laugh, we get drunk, we mingle with people from all social backgrounds...

Sounds like a dream, doesn't it? Don't get excited, it's not the 20th century anymore!

Today it's slightly different... We no longer mix poor and rich; girls must be beautiful and men rich.
A selection is done in front of each nightclub, from the simple pub to the fancy club.

Here are the instructions for getting into a nightclub and if possible, leaving with someone!

Have a great night, have fun (not too much, remember you are in Paris!)

PRACTICAL INFORMATION

• **Opening hours:**
Open from 11pm for Provincials; Parisians arrive around 2am, when the bars have closed.

• **Where?**
Bastille, Châtelet, Montparnasse, le Marais, Oberkampf and Mouffetard (the Cougars' paradise), Quartier Latin, Grands Boulevards, Pigalle, Montmartre.

• **When?**
From Thursday to Saturday.

• **Dress code :**
(skip this part if you go to a libertine club)

Woman:
Sexy without being vulgar.
Light makeup.
Black dress slightly above the knee.
High heels.

Man:
Dress as you would in the middle of the day:
dark jeans, black or grey shirt, smart shoes.
Trainers are not allowed!

If you live in a small town, you will be shocked by the difference between an evening in Province and in Paris:

In Roubaix (north of France) when you go to a club, you rarely ask yourself the question: "Will I be denied access?" You have other concerns:

- 7:45pm you buy a bottle of whiskey and coke.
- 8:00pm you eat.
- 9:00pm you start drinking.
- 10:00pm you take your car.
- 10:01pm you meet a policeman who is also your neighbour.
- 10:02pm you arrive at the parking lot.
- 10:03pm you drink the bottle you bought at the supermarket at 7:45pm in the car, with your friends.
- 11pm you kiss the bouncer Regis and Lisi at the cloakroom.
- 11pm/5am you're having fun.

In Paris, when you arrive at the nightclub, you have to face the almighty God of Parisian nights: The Bouncer.
If you have never been confronted with him, know that it is a human being, often wider than tall, who can ruin your evening with merely a look and a sentence (often short).
The bouncer never smiles, unless you're a girl with a plunging neckline, showing your belly button.

If you're a woman, he is unlikely to refuse you entry because even if you don't look like a Moldovan model, someone will want you at 5am.

You have a nice bank account, you like to drink and you're not stingy? You will be welcomed as a king or queen. Run to the VIP lounge, the waitress is already waiting for you with the card machine!

If you're a man, arriving alone - or worse, with a group of male friends - the bouncer already has his comments prepared. Don't bother arguing, there's no chance you'll get in:

"Tu a l'air fatigué !" ("You look tired!") ➔ the bouncer politely tells you that you've obviously had too many drinks. You have the right to be an alcoholic, but only inside.

"Ça ne va pas être possible !" ("It's not going to be possible!") ➔ this is a definite NO.

"C'est réservé aux habitués !" ("It's for regulars only!") ➔ Avoid answering like a provincial: ***"Si je ne rentre pas je ne serai jamais habitué"*** ("If I can't get in, I'll never be a regular").
It's pointless because they simply don't want people like you!

To avoid this humiliation, grab a group of young girls, post-puberty age, by promising them a Mojito. You're never too young to learn the art of bribery!
Congratulations, you've passed the bouncer test!

Once inside, start by having a drink at the bar. Make sure the bartender pours you the right amount of alcohol and gives you the correct amount of change. You should trust the bartender about as much as you can trust a bulimic friend with your Serrano ham and mozzarella sandwich.

Sip your cocktail while watching people. Don't forget to criticize them:

"How can she wear that dress with the legs she has?"

"Oh là là, check out this girl dancing,
I'm sure she's from Province!"

"Look at the other American girl with her pole dancing bar between her buttocks, she doesn't even respect herself anymore!"

"Even she has a boyfriend!"

A few drinks later, brave the dance floor, but avoid smiling at people because they are not there to socialise. Don't forget to take a selfie and post it on social media, and don't be afraid to lie:
#craziness #fun #party #parisjetaime.

If you ever want to find your soul mate, here's my advice:

If you're a woman and you want to hit on a Parisian: one smile and he's yours!
The task will be much more complicated if you're a man.
You're not a fighter? You will easily find a tourist who's flying home the next day, with no time to waste.

In my opinion; if you like a challenge, get closer to a Parisian woman.

How to recognize her?

If you see a woman looking arrogant, she's no doubt Parisian!! Don't forget that the Parisian woman is suspicious, independent and demanding, so... single. She doesn't come to a nightclub to meet her soulmate, she's there to forget her hard week at work. However, she remains a sexual being, so you have a (tiny) chance of scoring. Choose a 40-year-old woman, she will be easier to tame because her biological clock is still ticking, but her batteries will soon be dead.

As soon as you find her, keep your distance because the Parisian woman has claustrophobic tendencies. Stay three metres away from her. Don't stare at her too much because she'll think you're a pervert or a Provincial. After a few minutes, offer her a glass of champagne. If she says no: give up...

One day, you can tell your children:

"I've done a lot of things in my life,
I even hit on a Parisian woman...".

To forget this crushing blow, order a drink at the bar and head to the dance floor, close your eyes and let your body express itself...

BACK TO REALITY

It is 4:45 am, the volume of the music fades, the lights come on again, a feeling of calm and serenity overwhelms you, suddenly the bouncer (and his kind hospitality) shouts: "We're closed, get out!"

It's 5am, you're sleepy, but Paris is waking up. All you have to do now is bankrupt yourself on a VTC to get home or go and wait forever for the first subway... It's up to you!

Good night!

8. HAVING A CHILD IN PARIS

- *I'd prefer it inside !*

After spending a few years with your partner, what could be more logical than wanting to start a family?

Parisian life is very intense but can become even more so with the arrival of a child.

During pregnancy, you will ask yourself the crucial question: ***"Where will we put it?"***

Don't panic, you have nine months to get organised!

Come on, let's get to work!

If you come from Province, you know the "ideal" life scenario:

A couple at 16, engaged at 18, married at 24, owner of a house at 25, you conceive a child the same evening you get the keys to your new house. The baby room is ready and decorated on the day of your first scan, you're fed up at 30 and you divorce at 40! All happiness!

In Paris, it's radically different! You enjoy your youth, you go out, you flirt, you make a career plan, your life goes by at a crazy speed, you celebrate your 35th birthday and then you realise that you forgot to reproduce. No stress, nature is still here for a few more years.

IN UTERO

When you are ready to become a parent, fill in your nursery application and mail it the same day you get a positive pregnancy test result, because there are not enough spaces for everyone!

Increase your chances of getting a place in a nursery by conceiving your child in September. He will be born in June, perfect timing for the start of the school year!

In a worst case scenario, you can use a nanny, but it's wiser to trust a business than a human being. If you're not convinced, go for a walk in the public gardens, where you'll see many "nannies" more interested in the number of "likes" of their Facebook status than in the child, who has already swallowed 8 cigarette butts, licked 6 pigeon feathers and eaten a handful of sand.

THE BIRTH

9 months later, the baby is finally here!
What a great joy, your couple becomes a family!
As soon as you get out of the maternity ward, get a taxi home. Keep your baby from vomiting on the taxi seats, or you might end up walking to your house!
If your baby cries, comfort him and explain that she was born in the most beautiful city in the world. The sound of the engine and horns should calm her down, until the driver screams: ***"Putain, avance connard !"*** ("Fuck, come on, asshole!")

THE RETURN HOME

When you arrive at your building, don't be surprised if your neighbours don't look enthusiastic... they would have preferred you to be sterile!

If you have a touch of humour, stick a letter on the elevator door:

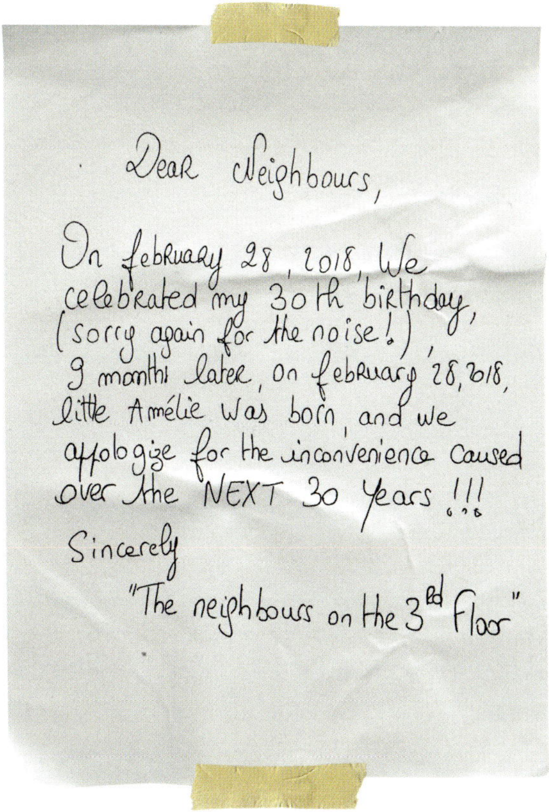

Dear Neighbours,

On february 28, 2018, We
celebrated my 30th birthday,
(sorry again for the noise!),
9 months later, on february 28, 2018,
little Amélie was born, and we
appologize for the inconvenience caused
over the NEXT 30 Years !!!

Sincerely

"The neighbours on the 3rd Floor"

When you get to your apartment, introduce her to it. As you already know, apartments in Paris are ridiculously small... so the tour won't take long.

When the child is three months old (if you're still together), it's time to put your child in a nursery and get your life back.

ON THE MOVE WITH A BABY

To move around with your baby, the options are quite limited:

• **The metro:**

Do you have masochistic tendencies? Then this is the means of transport for you!
Dozens of steps to go up and down with the stroller, plus unbearable heat. Just forget about it!

• **The bus:**

A rather practical means of transport, however, there is no room for more than 2 strollers at a time!
If you are antisocial (therefore "Parisian"), the journey can turn into an ordeal when some elderly people, missing their grandchildren, start stroking your child's cheeks without any embarrassment! A real ordeal!

• **On foot:**

This is the best way to travel with a child. However, given how narrow some pavements are, opt for a stroller that is only slightly wider than her chest.
Avoid walking around at rush hour, because you'll piss everyone off: ***"Rrrrr, fait chier ces poussettes !"*** ("Rrrrrr, fuck these strollers!").

THE DISCOVERY OF PARIS

The seasons and childhood illnesses are moving so fast.
Your previous life without a kid: **work / cocktails / dodo (sleeping) has turned into a metro / nursery / work / metro / paediatrician / pharmacy / Hôpital Necker (hospital for kids) / sleepless nights.**

18 months have passed, your baby is taking her first steps... Here comes the magical period of parks and sandpits… one of the only (unavoidable) moments when you envy your Provincial friend's garden. You are divided between the desire to throw yourself under a metro train, and the joy of your child discovering nature.

Take advantage of your walk so she can discover the Parisian fauna: ducks, ponies, mice, rats and pigeons...

Teach your child the fear of others: ***"Ne parle pas aux inconnus"*** ("Don't talk to strangers"), a sentence that still resonates in the adult Parisian's head.

Warn your child about the world around her: ***"attention à la marche, attention aux voitures, attention au chien, attention aux vélos, attention aux crottes de chien, attention aux gens"***... ("Watch out for the step, the cars, the dog, the bikes, the dog poo")...

After having taken care of your baby for many months, it's time to get back into the real Parisian way of life...

FIRST RESTAURANT WITH BABY

In many countries, dinner at a restaurant with your child is common. In Paris, it's radically different: your child is persona non grata.
Do you doubt it? Try!

As soon as you get there, ask for a high chair! The server will be upset by your request, and will answer you with the greatest contempt: ***"Beh, non !"*** ("Of course, not!") There's only one option left: your kid will eat on your lap. The waiter will be so happy because you will only use a table for two!

Then ask the waiter if the restaurant offers a children's menu. He'll answer you with an arrogant smile: ***"Beh, non !"*** ("Beh, of course not!").

Does your child need to be changed? Go to the basement toilet, look for the changing table, and look very carefully - because you will never find it!

If your child makes a fuss or talks too loudly, don't make eye contact with the customers at nearby tables, because they are mad at you for ruining their evening!

The restaurant experience ends with an aftertaste of incomprehension.
Am I the only one who loves children?
Yes, yes, yes - you are!

Parisian restaurant owners love children - as long as they stay inside their mother's womb!

The life of a parent is tough in Paris! If you're financially comfortable, take advantage of it to get some breathing space for yourself and your little family!

Why don't we go on holiday?

9. THE PARISIAN ON HOLIDAY

#disconnect #instantfamily

After a few months of hard work, pressure and stress have become your best friends!
You are irritated, exhausted, depressed and even suicidal if you work in marketing, communication or digital...

A few litres of under eye concealer later, the burn-out knocks at your door... Don't open it! Send it to Japan or the United States instead! It will be more successful because in these countries, people have less than 2 weeks of holidays... they don't even dare to take them... it's frowned upon to think of yourself!

Don't worry, it'll never happen in France! Parisians have over 30 days of annual leave! They are entitled to it, so they take them! So enjoy it, pack your bags and fly away from the Capital... to come back with a fresh new perspective.

Enjoy your holidays....

ON WEEK-ENDS

From January, check the calendar carefully to plan your extended weekends in May. Pray as much as you can that this year's bank holidays don't fall on a weekend!

Only 2 hours from Paris by train, Deauville is THE destination for the "perfect" Parisian.
You won't feel lost because there are many people, it's very expensive and it's full of Parisians. Deauville is the 21st arrondissement of Paris.

• **Dress code:**
Mariniere (dark blue and white striped shirt), jeans and wellies.

• **Food**
Don't forget to eat like everyone else: cream mussels and French fries for lunch and a seafood platter in the evening.

Once the weekend is over, it will take you 4 hours to drive back to Paris by car!

Do you prefer more natural places, but still be surrounded by Parisians?
Choose Brittany, Vendée, or elsewhere in Normandy.

The idea of going to Province gives you psoriasis?
Take a city break in
Barcelona, Berlin, Rome, London, Lisbon.
No more than 3 days; because it's nice, but it's not Paris!

SUMMER HOLIDAYS

Now comes the most anticipated time of the year: the summer holidays!
Goodbye stress, public transport, pollution, work, noise... and Parisians.

- **So where to go?**

YOU ARE…	DESTINATION…
Rich	South-East / Corsica / Ile de Ré / La Baule / Ile d'Yeu
Bobo/écolo	Cap Ferret/ Biarritz / Ardèche/ Massif central / Bretagne
Broke	Aquaboulevard / Paris Plage

THE TYPICAL DAY OF THE PARISIAN AT THE BEACH

Barely awake, hurry up! Just the thought of doing nothing gives you a panic attack!

If you have a phone signal, take the opportunity to check the weather in Paris, and be happy if you have left your colleagues in the rain.

Go for a coffee on the terrace. As soon as the waiter gives you the bill, exclaim: ***"1 euro 20 le café ! On se fait vraiment entuber à Paris !"*** ("1 euro 20 per coffee! We really get screwed in Paris!").

When you get to the beach, take off your shoes, put your feet in the sand and say: ***"Oh, on se sent tellement libre"*** ("Oh, I feel so free").

Head to where there are the most people. If people are there, there must be a reason!
Put your towel down a few centimetres from another beachgoer, it irritates him but the promiscuity reassures you.
When you go swimming, complain about the temperature and cleanliness of the water, don't lose good habits.

A few minutes later, go back to your towel, shake it well without worrying about the people around you. If anyone dares to make a remark, say to him: ***"Je ne contrôle pas le vent !"*** ("I can't control the wind"!)

The Parisian pays attention to his skin, so think about protecting it.
Peeled face = useless holidays!
Don't forget that sunscreen makes your skin sticky, so as soon as your hand touches the sand, exclaim: ***"rrrrrooo c'est chiant tout ce sable !"*** ("rrrrrooo it's so annoying with all this sand!")

Relax by looking at your phone and in case of a non-existent signal, grumble: ***"Putain, mais c'est fou, même pas en Edge !"*** ("Fuck, it's crazy, not even an Edge signal!").

Take a picture of your feet with the sea in the background and post it on social media.

There's a good chance a child will whip you with sand while running for a swim. Scream out your annoyance: ***"Putain de gamin !"*** ("Fucking kid!")

When the sun starts to fade slightly, pack up your stuff because you can't tan after 7pm!

On the way back, stop in front of a real estate agency and compare the price of the properties with those in Paris: ***"Oh là là, tu as vu la maison avec piscine, c'est le prix d'un souplex de 11 mètres carrés à Belleville"*** ("Oh là là, you see this house with the swimming pool, it's the price of 11 square metres in Belleville!").
It's cheaper, but what anguish to live there all year round!

Come on, don't waste any more time; go take a shower, because the restaurant kitchen closes at 8pm! Be careful, don't just pick your restaurant at random. Check TripAdvisor to make sure this restaurant deserves you.

WINTER HOLIDAYS IN THE SUN

Flying to a sunny holiday destination during the winter is a MUST for a Parisian.
The privileged Parisians go to Thailand, Mexico, Bali, Miami, Costa Rica, Mauritius or the Dominican Republic.

Your first objective is to come home tanned enough to make all your colleagues jealous.
Post a picture of yourself in front of a heavenly setting on social media, to show your virtual friends how magical your life is.

Your hash tags	What your "friends" think when they stay in Paris
#jetlag	You deserve it!
#onestbien *(we feel so good)*	Bitch!
#jaitropchaud *(I'm too hot)*	Good for you, bitch!
#jaiprisuncoupdesoleil *(I've got a sunburn)*	I can't wait for your sunstroke!
#jevouslaissejevaismebaigner *(sorry, I have to go swimming)*	Hope you get eaten by a shark!
#derniercoucherdesoleil *(last sunset)*	Time to come home, bitch!
#danslaviondu retour *(on the plane coming back)*	Hope your skin starts peeling.
#voilacestfini *(that's the end)*	Time to come back to your shitty life!

Holiday over, return to the capital!
That breath of fresh air was great, but you missed Paris.
Let's get back to the real civilization!

The training is over !
Have you become a real Parisian?

10. THE PARISIAN QUIZ

- Oops...I'm wearing black from now on !

Here are 12 questions. Please tick an answer:

1) A woman gives birth on the metro:

☐ A You call the ambulance

☐ B You'll hold her hand

☐ C You ignore her, she could have a baby somewhere else, right?

2) An old man falls from the top of the metro stairs:

☐ A You run to his rescue

☐ B You start laughing

☐ C You take a picture of him to put him on Instagram **#rip #funerals**

3) A tourist seems lost:

☐ A You help him

☐ B You ignore him

☐ C You give him the wrong direction... it's not very nice, but it's funny!

4) When you arrive on the metro platform, a man throws himself under the train:

☐ A You're devastated, poor man!

☐ B It's sad, but you're going to be late

☐ C "Oh fuck! He had a shitty life, but he didn't have to piss everyone off!"

5) In a restaurant, a couple sits next to your table with their newborn baby:

☐ A Your hand is ready to wave hello as soon as he wakes up!
☐ B You just hope the infant will be quiet
☐ C You ask the waiter to change tables!

6) You take your dog for a walk when he suddenly does his business on a building:

☐ A You clean up, it's obvious!
☐ B You turn around... if no one has seen you, walk away!
☐ C You're not going to bend down to pick up your dog's trophy. That's what taxes are for, right?

7) What is your ideal outfit for a hot summer evening?

☐ A Bare-chested
☐ B Light clothing, shorts or skirt, short sleeve t-shirt
☐ C Trousers, long sleeve t-shirt and a scarf because you are never safe from a gust of wind.

8) At the bar, you order:

☐ A Whiskey & Coke
☐ B Vodka & Red Bull
☐ C White wine from the Loire valley (organic, sulphite-free), bought at your local wine shop (caviste)

9) You sit down on a terrace and the pint is 8 euros:

☐ A Outraged, you order a coffee!
☐ B You order one: it's expensive, but you're thirsty.
☐ C You tell all your friends because it's a good deal!

10) When you're in Province, you are:

☐ A At home

☐ B Happy to discover the life of farmers

☐ C Shocked because the restaurant's kitchen closes at 8pm

11) Driving in Paris is:

☐ A An ordeal

☐ B Practical

☐ C It's easy, but what the hell are these bikes doing?

12) Paris Plages (every August, the mayor of Paris opens the Seine river sidewalk and calls it "the Paris beach) is:

☐ A Wonderful!

☐ B A beautiful outdoor outing

☐ C The last step before hell

IF YOU TICKED MOSTLY...

A's: Provincial you are, Provincial you will stay.

B's: It's not bad, but you can do better!
I suggest you read this guide again.

C's: Congratulations, you are a real Parisian!
To validate this training, come and get your diploma
from the real Parisian at the end of my show
"How to Become a Parisian in One Hour?"

THIS

IS

JUST A...

GOOD BYE

I hope this guide gave you the keys to survive in this Parisian jungle!
More than 10 years ago, I was like you: a new Parisian.
I was afraid of this crazy life. Everything was going much too fast, people were always in a hurry.

After a few weeks, I started to love this new life.
Today, I can't imagine leaving this city because Paris is MY city!
My friends living in Province always ask me the same question:

"But how can you live in Paris?"

So I answer them that...

- I♥ to watch this rabbit get his fingers caught between the metro doors.
- I♥ to buy a hot baguette at any time of the day and eat half of it before going home.
- I♥ to eat Chinese in the 13th arrondissement and Indian in the 10th.
- I♥ the smile of the Parisian as the snow falls; and his irritation when it melts.
- I♥ the small boats floating on the fountain of the Luxembourg garden.
- I♥ to ask myself the question: "Do couples who place a lock on the bridge remove it when they split up?"
- I♥ to see people miss the last metro train of the evening.
- I♥ this old man who feeds the pigeons in front of the Georges Pompidou centre.

•I♥ to take the Montmartre funicular and tell myself that I did well (222 steps)!
•I♥ to think it's raining when it's a lady watering her geraniums.
•I♥ to land in Orly or Charles de Gaulle when I come home from holidays, finally at home!
•I♥ the first minutes of every hour when the Eiffel tower lights up.
•I♥ to hate Paris Plages.
•I♥ to say hello from a bridge, to the tourists who are on a Seine river cruise.
•I♥ to drink coffee on a terrace, and I like it even more when served with a speculoos.
•I♥ the sunset from the Pont Neuf.
•I♥ to see Parisians drink rosé as soon as it's 16 degrees.
•I♥ to see alcoholic Parisians complaining that they no longer have a place to party.
•I♥ to hear PSG supporters shout: PARIS IS MAGIC!
•I♥ to love Paris and I hope you will like it too!

See you soon... on stage or elsewhere...

TIME
TO SAY...

THANK
YOU

Thank you to my grandfather Antonio who would have celebrated his 100th birthday on the day of the book's publication.

Thank you for...ALL to my incredible and fabulous Claudie.
Thanks to my daughter Lily (my little golden heart that shines), Mom, Dad, Alain, Catherine, my sister and her childrens, Paulo, Claude, Evelyne, Ben.
Thank you to all my friends and family.
Thank you to Michèle Auffret for your precious help.
Thanks to Solène Debiès for the sumptuous illustrations.
Thanks to Guillaume Saix (webmyart) for the beautiful graphics.
Thanks to Elin Beckmann Britt, Richard and Olivia.
Thanks to Claire Waddington.
Thanks to Kevin Knight for your support !
Thanks to Maria Pipaud, Pascal Legros and the entire team at Théâtre des Nouveautés.
Thanks to Elisabeth Deswarte, Christine Malesieux, Vincent Dupuy, Marie Auburtin, Céline Février, Nancy Van Kuler, Marianne Bp, Cécile Leroux, Delphine Pommereul.
Thank you to the provincials for treating us with your cherry tomatoes from the garden: Solenn, Davy, Yuna, Deborah, Bruno, Jade and Noah. So much work and water for 8 cherry tomatoes!
Thank you to my loyal friends Facebook, Instagram and Twitter for being present for more than 10 years...
Thank you to Parisians, provincial, foreigners... You are my source of inspiration !

Thank you... to ME ! *(cf page 15: the Parisian is arrogant!)*

ABOUT THE AUTHOR...

OLIVIER GIRAUD

At the age of 8, Olivier Giraud already yearned to be on stage but, as far as his parents were concerned, earning a living as a comedian was beyond his reach. So Olivier decided to put that passion on the back burner, knowing full well that one day he would come back to his first dream: the stage.

In his teens he discovered a second passion and decided to become a chef. A few years later he graduated from a top French culinary arts school: Ferrandi. In 2001, Olivier packed his bags. His destination was the United States. He obtained a six-year visa and soon became Maître d' at one of the most prestigious hotels on the East Coast: The Breakers in Palm Beach, Florida.

And yet his childhood dream remained intact so he decided to return to Paris and try his luck in the spotlight. During his time working in service, he used to have a chuckle over the cultural contrasts between Americans and the French. Then one day he came up with the idea of writing a one-man show about all these differences. Olivier made a bold choice and wrote his show in English in order to be able to have an audience made up of spectators from all different horizons.

He presented his project to numerous showbiz professionals looking for their support but they all seemed to think it was doomed to failure. Since no one was prepared to take a gamble on him, he decided to put together his own production company: French Arrogance Production.

May 10th, 2009, "How to Become a Parisian in one Hour ?" was performed on stage for the first time.

In June 2014, Olivier Giraud was invited by the Bristish Embassy in Paris and introduced to Her Majesty The Queen Of England Elizabeth II. The invitation was in honor of his "contribution to Franco-British entente".

May 20th, 2016, he performed his show at the Olympia to celebrate the show's seventh anniversary. During those seven years the show had been performed 1,200 times in front of half a million people.

In 2016 and 2017, the show was voted Best comedy show in Paris" by expatriates living in the capital as part of the "Best in Paris" awards.

In March 2017, Olivier Giraud was invited by the Duke and Duchess of Cambridge to the British Embassy in Paris. At a cocktail reception for 100 of the most promising French entrepreneurs, he discussed the success of his show 100% in english with Her Royal Highness Kate Middleton.

November 28th, 2018, he published the book that you hold on your hands "How to become a Parisian in one hour?".

"Learning to Be French Through Comedy !"
THE NEW YORK TIMES
★★★★★

"The audience is in tears of laughter !"
TIME OUT
★★★★★

"Worldwide audience in a packed theater"
PLAYBILL
★★★★★

"The expert on Parisian behavior"
CNN
★★★★★

"A must see In Paris"
ELLE
★★★★★

Author : Olivier Giraud
www.oliviergiraud.com

@howtobecomeparisian

@parisianonehour

@OlivierGiraudOff

@TheFRENCHARROGANCE

Illustrated by Solène Debiès
Designed by Guillaume Saix (webmyart)
Photo cover : Charles Roux
Photo back cover : Julia Griner
Photo author's biography : Claudie Pichon

PEFC 10-1-1

Printed in France by par Cloitre IMPRIMEURS
10 rue André Michelin – 29170 Saint-Évarzec
Achevé d'imprimer : november 2018
Dépôt légal : october 2018